Hamlet

For Schools and Performance

By

William Shakespeare

Abridged by KJ O'Hara

ISBN: 978-1546574293
Published by Antic Mind
102 Dudwell Lane, Halifax, UK. HX30SH
All Enquiries to publisher@anticmind.com

Contents

Forward

In abridging Hamlet for schools and performance I have brought together my experience as a former artistic director of a theatre in education company and of being an English and drama teacher for over 25 years.

Hamlet is, arguably, Shakespeare's greatest play: rich in plot, character and language. At around 30,000 words, it is also his longest, taking around four hours to perform. My aim, therefore, was to produce a shortened version (this version is around 17,000 words) which would improve the accessibility of the play to a younger audience without taking anything away from the amazing story which unfolds.

In abridging this text, I have ensured that the all the essential elements of the play remain completely intact: the plot and subplots remain coherent, characters are fully developed and all the text is original. It still contains everything an English teacher would want to see in order to carry out a detailed study and its major speeches have been left untouched.

I have used this version in both English and drama lessons, refining it over the years. It's a version that young people can access and enjoy, it provides opportunity for dramatic exploration and performance, and it remains detailed enough for high school level, English analysis.

KJ O'Hara

Dramatis Personae

Claudius:	King of Denmark
Hamlet:	Son to the late and nephew to the present king
Polonius:	Lord Chamberlain
Horatio:	Friend to Hamlet
Laertes:	Son to Polonius

Voltimand, Cornelius, Rosencrantz, Guildenstern, Osric, a Gentleman: Courtiers

A Priest

Marcellus, Barnardo:	Officers
Francisco:	A soldier

Players

Two Clowns:	Grave-diggers
Fortinbras:	Prince of Norway
Gertrude:	Queen of Denmark and mother to Hamlet
Ophelia:	Daughter to Polonius

Lords, Ladies, Officers, Soldiers, Sailors, Messengers, and other Attendants

Ghost of Hamlet's Father

ACT I

Act I Scene I

Elsinore. A platform before the castle.

FRANCISCO at his post. Enter BERNARDO.

BERNARDO	Who's there?
FRANCISCO	Nay, answer me: stand, and unfold yourself.
BERNARDO	Long live the king!
FRANCISCO	Bernardo?
BERNARDO	He.
FRANCISCO	You come most carefully upon your hour.
BERNARDO	'Tis now struck twelve; get thee to bed, Francisco.
FRANCISCO	For this relief much thanks: 'tis bitter cold, And I am sick at heart.
BERNARDO	Have you had quiet guard?
FRANCISCO	Not a mouse stirring.
BERNARDO	Well, good night.

Exit FRANSISCO. Enter HORATIO and MARCELLUS

BERNARDO	Welcome, Horatio: welcome, good Marcellus.
MARCELLUS	What, has this thing appear'd again to-night?
BERNARDO	I have seen nothing.
MARCELLUS	Horatio says 'tis but our fantasy, Therefore I have entreated him along That if again this apparition come, He may approve our eyes and speak to it.

HORATIO	Tush, tush, 'twill not appear.
BERNARDO	Sit down awhile; And let us once again assail your ears, That are so fortified against our story What we have two nights seen.
HORATIO	Well, sit we down, And let us hear Bernardo speak of this.

Enter Ghost

MARCELLUS	Peace, look, where it comes again!
BERNARDO	In the same figure, like the king that's dead.
MARCELLUS	Thou art a scholar; speak to it, Horatio.
BERNARDO	Looks it not like the king? mark it, Horatio.
HORATIO	Most like: it harrows me with fear and wonder.
BERNARDO	It would be spoke to.
MARCELLUS	Question it, Horatio.
HORATIO	What art thou that usurp'st this time of night, Together with that fair and warlike form In which the majesty of buried Denmark Did sometimes march? by heaven I charge thee, speak!
MARCELLUS	It is offended.
BERNARDO	See, it stalks away!
HORATIO	Stay! speak, speak! I charge thee, speak!

Exit Ghost

MARCELLUS	'Tis gone, and will not answer.
BERNARDO	How now, Horatio! you tremble and look pale: Is not this something more than fantasy?

HORATIO   Before my God, I might not this believe
Without the sensible and true avouch
Of mine own eyes.

MARCELLUS   Is it not like the king?

HORATIO   As thou art to thyself:
'Tis strange; But in the gross and scope of my opinion,
This bodes some strange eruption to our state.

MARCELLUS   Good now, sit down, and tell me, he that knows,
Why this same strict and most observant watch
So nightly toils the subject of the land,
And why such daily cast of brazen cannon,
And foreign mart for implements of war;
Who is't that can inform me?

HORATIO   That can I;
At least, the whisper goes so. Our last king,
Was, as you know, by Fortinbras of Norway,
Dared to the combat; in which our valiant Hamlet
Did slay this Fortinbras; who did forfeit,
With his life, all his lands to the conqueror.
Now, sir, young Fortinbras,
Of unimproved mettle hot and full,
Hath shark'd up a list of lawless resolutes,
to some enterprise that hath a stomach in't;
But to recover of us, by strong hand
And terms compulsatory, those foresaid lands
So by his father lost: and this, I take it,
Is the main motive of our preparations.

BERNARDO   I think it be no other but e'en so:
Well may it sort that this portentous figure
Comes armed through our watch; so like the king
That was and is the question of these wars.

HORATIO   A mote it is to trouble the mind's eye.
In the most high and palmy state of Rome,
A little ere the mightiest Julius fell,
The graves stood tenantless and the sheeted dead

Did squeak and gibber in the Roman streets:
But soft, behold! lo, where it comes again!

Re-enter Ghost

I'll cross it, though it blast me. Stay, illusion!
If thou hast any sound, or use of voice,
Speak to me:
If there be any good thing to be done,
That may to thee do ease and grace to me,
Speak to me:

Cock crows

If thou art privy to thy country's fate,
Which, happily, foreknowing may avoid, O, speak!
Stay, and speak! Stop it, Marcellus.

MARCELLUS   Shall I strike at it with my partisan?

HORATIO   Do, if it will not stand.

BERNARDO   'Tis here!

HORATIO   'Tis here!

MARCELLUS   'Tis gone!

Exit Ghost

We do it wrong, being so majestical,
To offer it the show of violence;
For it is, as the air, invulnerable,
And our vain blows malicious mockery.

BERNARDO   It was about to speak, when the cock crew.

HORATIO   And then it started like a guilty thing
Upon a fearful summons. I have heard,
The cock, that is the trumpet to the morn,
Doth awake the god of day; and, at his warning,
The extravagant and erring spirit hies
To his confine.

MARCELLUS   It faded on the crowing of the cock.
Some say that ever 'gainst that season comes
Wherein our Saviour's birth is celebrated,
The bird of dawning singeth all night long:

And then, they say, no spirit dares stir abroad;
The nights are wholesome; then no planets strike,
No fairy takes, nor witch hath power to charm,
So hallow'd and so gracious is the time.

HORATIO So have I heard and do in part believe it.
Let us impart what we have seen to-night
Unto young Hamlet; for, upon my life,
This spirit, dumb to us, will speak to him.

MARCELLUS Let's do't, I pray; and I this morning know
Where we shall find him most conveniently.

Exeunt

Act I Scene II

A room of state in the castle.

Enter KING CLAUDIUS, QUEEN GERTRUDE, HAMLET, POLONIUS, LAERTES, VOLTIMAND, CORNELIUS, Lords, and Attendants

KING CLAUDIUS	Though yet of Hamlet our dear brother's death
	The memory be green, and that it us befitted
	To bear our hearts in grief
	Yet so far hath discretion fought with nature
	That we with wisest sorrow think on him,
	Together with remembrance of ourselves.
	Therefore our sometime sister, now our queen,
	The imperial jointress to this warlike state,
	Have we, taken to wife. Now follows,
	That you know, young Fortinbras,
	Holding a weak supposal of our worth,
	Hath not fail'd to pester us with message,
	Importing the surrender of those lands
	Lost by his father. We have here writ
	To Norway, uncle of young Fortinbras,
	To suppress his further gait herein;
	And we here dispatch
	You, good Cornelius, and you, Voltimand,
	For bearers of this greeting to old Norway;
	Farewell, and let your haste commend your duty.

Exeunt VOLTIMAND and CORNELIUS

	And now, Laertes, you told us of some suit;
	What wouldst thou beg, Laertes?
LAERTES	My dread lord,
	Your leave and favour to return to France;
	From whence though willingly I came to Denmark,
	To show my duty in your coronation.
KING CLAUDIUS	Have you your father's leave? What says Polonius?
LORD POLONIUS	He hath, my lord, wrung from me my slow leave
	I do beseech you, give him leave to go.

KING CLAUDIUS	Take thy fair hour, Laertes; time be thine,
	And thy best graces spend it at thy will!
	But now, my cousin Hamlet, and my son,--
HAMLET	[Aside] A little more than kin, and less than kind.
KING CLAUDIUS	How is it that the clouds still hang on you?
HAMLET	Not so, my lord; I am too much i' the sun.
QUEEN GERTRUDE	Good Hamlet, cast thy nighted colour off,
	And let thine eye look like a friend on Denmark.
	Do not for ever with thy vailed lids
	Seek for thy noble father in the dust:
	Thou know'st 'tis common; all that lives must die,
	Passing through nature to eternity.
HAMLET	Ay, madam, it is common.
QUEEN GERTRUDE	If it be,
	Why seems it so particular with thee?
HAMLET	Seems, madam! nay it is; I know not 'seems.'
	'Tis not alone my inky cloak, good mother,
	Nor customary suits of solemn black,
	That can denote me truly: these indeed seem,
	For they are actions that a man might play:
	But I have that within which passeth show;
	These but the trappings and the suits of woe.
KING CLAUDIUS	'Tis sweet and commendable in your nature, Hamlet,
	To give these mourning duties to your father:
	But, to persever is a course
	Of impious stubbornness; 'tis unmanly grief;
	Fie! 'tis a fault to heaven, a fault against the dead.
	We pray you, throw to earth
	This unprevailing woe, and think of us
	As of a father: for let the world take note,
	You are the most immediate to our throne;
	And with no less nobility of love
	Than that which dearest father bears his son,

Do I impart toward you. For your intent
In going back to school in Wittenberg,
It is most retrograde to our desire:
And we beseech you, bend you to remain
Here, in the cheer and comfort of our eye,
Our chiefest courtier, cousin, and our son.

QUEEN GERTRUDE   Let not thy mother lose her prayers, Hamlet:
I pray thee, stay with us; go not to Wittenberg.

HAMLET   I shall in all my best obey you, madam.

KING CLAUDIUS   Why, 'tis a loving and a fair reply:
Madam, come; this gentle and unforced
Accord of Hamlet Sits smiling to my heart:
Come away.

Exeunt all but HAMLET

HAMLET   O, that this too too solid flesh would melt
Thaw and resolve itself into a dew!
Or that the Everlasting had not fix'd
His canon 'gainst self-slaughter! O God! God!
How weary, stale, flat and unprofitable,
Seem to me all the uses of this world!
Fie on't! ah fie! 'tis an unweeded garden,
That grows to seed; things rank and gross in nature
Possess it merely. That it should come to this!
But two months dead: nay, not so much, not two:
So excellent a king; that was, to this,
Hyperion to a satyr; so loving to my mother
That he might not beteem the winds of heaven
Visit her face too roughly. Heaven and earth!
Must I remember? why, she would hang on him,
As if increase of appetite had grown
By what it fed on: and yet, within a month--
Let me not think on't--Frailty, thy name is woman!--
A little month, or ere those shoes were old
With which she follow'd my poor father's body,
Like Niobe, all tears:--why she, even she--
O, God! a beast, that wants discourse of reason,
Would have mourn'd longer--married with my uncle,

My father's brother, but no more like my father
Than I to Hercules: within a month:
Ere yet the salt of most unrighteous tears
Had left the flushing in her galled eyes,
She married. O, most wicked speed, to post
With such dexterity to incestuous sheets!
It is not nor it cannot come to good:
But break, my heart; for I must hold my tongue.

Enter HORATIO, MARCELLUS, and BERNARDO

HORATIO   Hail to your lordship!

HAMLET   Horatio,--or I do forget myself.
What is your affair in Elsinore?
We'll teach you to drink deep ere you depart.

HORATIO   My lord, I came to see your father's funeral.

HAMLET   I pray thee, do not mock me, fellow-student;
I think it was to see my mother's wedding.

HORATIO   Indeed, my lord, it follow'd hard upon.

HAMLET   Thrift, thrift, Horatio! the funeral baked meats
Did coldly furnish forth the marriage tables.
My father!--methinks I see my father.

HORATIO   Where, my lord?

HAMLET   In my mind's eye, Horatio.
He was a man, take him for all in all,
I shall not look upon his like again.

HORATIO   My lord, I think I saw him yesternight.

HAMLET   For God's love, let me hear.

HORATIO   Two nights together had these gentlemen,
Marcellus and Bernardo, on their watch,
In the dead vast and middle of the night,
Been thus encounter'd. A figure like your father,
Armed at point exactly, appears before them.

This to me in dreadful secrecy impart they did;
And I with them the third night kept the watch;
Where the apparition comes: I knew your father;
These hands are not more like.

HAMLET   Did you not speak to it?

HORATIO   My lord, I did;
But answer made it none: yet once methought
It lifted up its head like as it would speak;
But even then the morning cock crew loud,
And at the sound it shrunk in haste away,
And vanish'd from our sight.

HAMLET   'Tis very strange. Arm'd, say you?

MARCELLUS   Arm'd, my lord.

BERNARDO   From head to foot.

HAMLET   I would I had been there. I will watch to-night;
Perchance 'twill walk again.

HORATIO   I warrant it will.

HAMLET   If it assume my noble father's person,
I'll speak to it, though hell itself should gape
And bid me hold my peace. I pray you all,
If you have hitherto conceal'd this sight,
Let it be tenable in your silence still;
And whatsoever else shall hap to-night,
Give it an understanding, but no tongue:
I will requite your loves. So, fare you well:
Upon the platform, 'twixt eleven and twelve,
I'll visit you.

All   Our duty to your honour.

Exeunt all but HAMLET

HAMLET My father's spirit in arms! all is not well;
I doubt some foul play: foul deeds will rise,
Though all the earth o'erwhelm them, to men's eyes.

Exit

Act I Scene III

A room in Polonius' house.

Enter LAERTES and OPHELIA

LAERTES
My necessaries are embark'd: farewell:
And, sister, let me hear from you.

OPHELIA
Do you doubt that?

LAERTES
For Hamlet and the trifling of his favour,
Hold it a fashion and a toy in blood, no more.
Perhaps he loves you now,
But his will is not his own;
For he himself is subject to his birth:
He may not, as unvalued persons do,
Carve for himself; for on his choice depends
The safety and health of this whole state.
Then if he says he loves you,
Weigh what loss your honour may sustain,
If with too credent ear you list his songs,
Or lose your heart, or your chaste treasure open
To his unmaster'd importunity.
Fear it, Ophelia, fear it, my dear sister,
And keep you in the rear of your affection,
Out of the shot and danger of desire.
I stay too long: but here my father comes.

Enter POLONIUS

LORD POLONIUS
Yet here, Laertes! aboard, aboard, for shame!
The wind sits in the shoulder of your sail,
And you are stay'd for. There; my blessing with thee!
And these few precepts in thy memory
See thou character. Give thy thoughts no tongue,
Nor any unproportioned thought his act.
Be thou familiar, but by no means vulgar.
Those friends thou hast, and their adoption tried,
Grapple them to thy soul with hoops of steel;
But do not dull thy palm with entertainment

Of each new-hatch'd, unfledged comrade. Beware
Of entrance to a quarrel, but being in,
Bear't that the opposed may beware of thee.
Give every man thy ear, but few thy voice;
Take each man's censure, but reserve thy judgment.
Costly thy habit as thy purse can buy,
But not express'd in fancy; rich, not gaudy;
For the apparel oft proclaims the man,
And they in France of the best rank and station
Are of a most select and generous chief in that.
Neither a borrower nor a lender be;
For loan oft loses both itself and friend,
And borrowing dulls the edge of husbandry.
This above all: to thine ownself be true,
And it must follow, as the night the day,
Thou canst not then be false to any man.
Farewell: my blessing season this in thee!

LAERTES   Most humbly do I take my leave, my lord.
                 Farewell, Ophelia; and remember well
                 What I have said to you.

Exit

LORD POLONIUS   What is't, Ophelia, he hath said to you?

OPHELIA   So please you, something touching the Lord Hamlet.

LORD POLONIUS   Marry, well bethought:
                 'Tis told me, he hath very oft of late
                 Given private time to you; and you yourself
                 Have of your audience been most free and bounteous:
                 If it be so, as so 'tis put on me,
                 And that in way of caution, I must tell you,
                 You do not understand yourself so clearly
                 As it behoves my daughter and your honour.
                 What is between you? give me up the truth.

OPHELIA   He hath, my lord, of late made many tenders
                 Of his affection to me.

LORD POLONIUS	Affection! pooh! you speak like a green girl,
	Unsifted in such perilous circumstance.
	Do you believe his tenders, as you call them?

| OPHELIA | I do not know, my lord, what I should think. |

LORD POLONIUS	Marry, I'll teach you: think yourself a baby;
	That you have ta'en these tenders for true pay,
	Which are not sterling. Tender yourself more dearly;
	Or you'll tender me a fool.

OPHELIA	My lord, he hath importuned me with love
	In honourable fashion.
	And hath given countenance to his speech, my lord,
	With almost all the holy vows of heaven.

LORD POLONIUS	Ay, springes to catch woodcocks. Ophelia,
	Do not believe his vows; I would not,
	In plain terms, from this time forth,
	Have you so slander any moment leisure,
	As to give words or talk with the Lord Hamlet.
	Look to't, I charge you: come your ways.

| OPHELIA | I shall obey, my lord. |

Exeunt

Act I Scene IV

The platform

Enter HAMLET, HORATIO, and MARCELLUS

HAMLET   What hour now?

HORATIO   I think it lacks of twelve.

HAMLET   No, it is struck.

HORATIO   Indeed? I heard it not: then it draws near the season
Wherein the spirit held his wont to walk.

A flourish of trumpets, and ordnance shot off, within

                      What does this mean, my lord?

HAMLET   The king doth wake to-night and takes his rouse,
Keeps wassail, and the swaggering up-spring reels;
And, as he drains his draughts of Rhenish down,
The kettle-drum and trumpet thus bray out
The triumph of his pledge.

HORATIO   Is it a custom?

HAMLET   Ay, marry, is't:
But to my mind, though I am native here
And to the manner born, it is a custom
More honour'd in the breach than the observance.
This heavy-headed revel east and west
Makes us traduced and tax'd of other nations:
They clepe us drunkards.

HORATIO   Look, my lord, it comes!

Enter Ghost

HAMLET   Angels and ministers of grace defend us!
Be thou a spirit of health or goblin damn'd,
Thou comest in such a questionable shape

That I will speak to thee: I'll call thee Hamlet,
King, father, royal Dane: O, answer me!
Let me not burst in ignorance; but tell
Why thy canonized bones, hearsed in death,
Have burst their cerements; What may this mean,
That thou, dead corse, again in complete steel
Revisit'st thus the glimpses of the moon.
Say, why is this? wherefore? what should we do?

Ghost beckons HAMLET

HORATIO   It beckons you to go away with it.

HAMLET   Then I will follow it.

HORATIO   Do not, my lord.

HAMLET   Why, what should be the fear?
I do not set my life in a pin's fee;
And for my soul, what can it do to that,
Being a thing immortal as itself?
It waves me forth again: I'll follow it.

MARCELLUS   You shall not go, my lord.

HAMLET   Hold off your hands.

HORATIO   Be ruled; you shall not go.

HAMLET   Unhand me, gentlemen.
By heaven, I'll make a ghost of him that lets me!

Exeunt Ghost and HAMLET

MARCELLUS   Something is rotten in the state of Denmark.
Let's follow him.

Exeunt

Act 1 Scene V

Another part of the platform.

Enter GHOST and HAMLET

HAMLET	Speak; I am bound to hear.
Ghost	So art thou to revenge, when thou shalt hear.
HAMLET	What?
Ghost	I am thy father's spirit,
	Doom'd for a certain term to walk the night,
	And for the day confined to fast in fires,
	Till the foul crimes done in my days of nature
	Are burnt and purged away. But list, O, list!
	If thou didst ever thy dear father love
	Revenge his foul and most unnatural murder.
HAMLET	Murder!
Ghost	Murder most foul, strange and unnatural.
HAMLET	Haste me to know't, that I, with wings as swift
	As meditation or the thoughts of love,
	May sweep to my revenge.
Ghost	I find thee apt. Now, Hamlet, hear:
	'Tis given out that, sleeping in my orchard,
	A serpent stung me; so the whole ear of Denmark
	Is by a forged process of my death
	Rankly abused: but know, thou noble youth,
	The serpent that did sting thy father's life
	Now wears his crown.
HAMLET	O my prophetic soul! My uncle!
Ghost	Ay, that incestuous, that adulterate beast,
	With witchcraft of his wit, with traitorous gifts
	Won to his shameful lust
	The will of my most seeming-virtuous queen:
	But, soft! Brief let me be. Sleeping within my orchard,

	Thy uncle stole, with juice of cursèd hebenon in a vial,
	And in the porches of my ears did pour
	The leperous distilment;
	Thus was I, sleeping, by a brother's hand
	Of life, of crown, of queen, at once dispatch'd:
	Cut off even in the blossoms of my sin,
	No reckoning made, but sent to my account
	With all my imperfections on my head:
	O, horrible! O, horrible! most horrible!
	If thou hast nature in thee, bear it not;
	Let not the royal bed of Denmark be
	A couch for luxury and damned incest.
	But, howsoever thou pursuest this act,
	Taint not thy mind, nor let thy soul contrive
	Against thy mother aught: leave her to heaven
	And to those thorns that in her bosom lodge,
	To prick and sting her. Fare thee well at once!
	Adieu, adieu! Hamlet, remember me.

Exit

HAMLET Remember thee!
Yea thy commandment all alone shall live
Within the book and volume of my brain,
O most pernicious woman!
O villain, villain, smiling, damned villain!
So, uncle, there you are. Now to my word;
It is 'Adieu, adieu! remember me.'
I have sworn 't.

Enter HORATIO and MARCELLUS

HORATIO What news, my lord?

HAMLET O, wonderful!

HORATIO Good my lord, tell it.

HAMLET No; you'll reveal it.

HORATIO Not I, my lord, by heaven.

MARCELLUS	Nor I, my lord.
HAMLET	There's ne'er a villain dwelling in all Denmark But he's an arrant knave. Touching this vision here, It is an honest ghost, that let me tell you: And now, good friends, give me one poor request.
HORATIO	What is't, my lord? we will.
HAMLET	Never make known what you have seen to-night.
HORATIO MARCELLUS	My lord, we will not.
HAMLET	Nay, but swear't. Upon my sword.
HORATIO	Propose the oath, my lord.
HAMLET	Never to speak of this that you have seen, Swear by my sword.
Ghost	[Beneath] Swear.
HORATIO	O day and night, but this is wondrous strange!
HAMLET	And therefore as a stranger give it welcome. There are more things in heaven and earth, Horatio, Than are dreamt of in your philosophy. But come; Here, as before, never, so help you mercy, How strange or odd soe'er I bear myself, As I perchance hereafter shall think meet To put an antic disposition on, That you, at such times seeing me, to note That you know aught of me: Swear.
Ghost	[Beneath] Swear.
They swear	
HAMLET	So, gentlemen, Let us go in together; And still your fingers on your lips, I pray. The time is out of joint: O cursed spite,

That ever I was born to set it right!
Nay, come, let's go together.

Exeunt

ACT II

Act II Scene I

A room in Polonius' house.

Enter OPHELIA

LORD POLONIUS How now, Ophelia! what's the matter?

OPHELIA O, my lord, my lord, I have been so affrighted!

LORD POLONIUS With what, i' the name of God?

OPHELIA My lord, as I was sewing in my closet,
Lord Hamlet, with his doublet all unbraced;
No hat upon his head; his stockings foul'd,
Ungarter'd, and down-gyved to his ancle;
Pale as his shirt; his knees knocking each other;
And with a look so piteous in purport
As if he had been loosed out of hell
To speak of horrors,--he comes before me.

LORD POLONIUS Mad for thy love?

OPHELIA My lord, I do not know; but truly, I do fear it.

LORD POLONIUS Come, go with me: I will go seek the king.
This is the very ecstasy of love,
Whose violent property fordoes itself
And leads the will to desperate undertakings
I am sorry. Have you given him any hard words of late?

OPHELIA No, my good lord, but, as you did command,
I did repel his fetters and denied
His access to me.

LORD POLONIUS That hath made him mad. I fear'd he did but trifle,
And meant to wreck thee; but, beshrew my jealousy!
Come, go we to the king: this must be known.

Exeunt

Act II Scene II

A room in the castle.

Enter KING CLAUDIUS, QUEEN GERTRUDE, ROSENCRANTZ, GUILDENSTERN, and Attendants

KING CLAUDIUS
Welcome, dear Rosencrantz and Guildenstern!
The need we have to use you did provoke
Our hasty sending. Something have you heard
Of Hamlet's transformation; What it should be,
More than his father's death, that thus hath put him
So much from the understanding of himself,
I cannot dream of: I entreat you both,
That you vouchsafe your rest here in our court
Some little time: so by your companies
To draw him on to pleasures, and to gather,
So much as from occasion you may glean,
Whether aught, to us unknown, afflicts him thus,
That, open'd, lies within our remedy.

QUEEN GERTRUDE
Good gentlemen,
Your visitation shall receive such thanks
As fits a king's remembrance.

GUILDENSTERN
We both obey, and here give up ourselves,
In the full bent to lay our service freely at your feet,
To be commanded.

KING CLAUDIUS
Thanks, Rosencrantz and gentle Guildenstern.

QUEEN GERTRUDE
Thanks, Guildenstern and gentle Rosencrantz:
And I beseech you instantly to visit
My too much changed son.

Exeunt ROSENCRANTZ, GUILDENSTERN, and some Attendants. Enter POLONIUS

LORD POLONIUS
The ambassadors from Norway, my good lord,
Are joyfully return'd.

KING CLAUDIUS
Thou still hast been the father of good news.

LORD POLONIUS
And I do think that I have found
The very cause of Hamlet's lunacy.

KING CLAUDIUS	O, speak of that; that do I long to hear.
LORD POLONIUS	Give first admittance to the ambassadors; My news shall be the fruit to that great feast.
KING CLAUDIUS	Thyself do grace to them, and bring them in.

Exit POLONIUS

He tells me, my dear Gertrude, he hath found
The head and source of all your son's distemper.

QUEEN GERTRUDE	I doubt it is no other but the main; His father's death, and our o'erhasty marriage.
KING CLAUDIUS	Well, we shall sift him.

Re-enter POLONIUS, with VOLTIMAND and CORNELIUS

Welcome, my good friends!
Say, Voltimand, what from our brother Norway?

VOLTIMAND	Most fair return of greetings and desires. He sends out arrests on Fortinbras; which he, in brief, obeys; Receives rebuke from Norway, and in fine Makes vow before his uncle never more To give the assay of arms against your majesty. Whereon old Norway, overcome with joy, Gives him commission to employ those soldiers, So levied as before, against the Polack: With an entreaty, herein further shown,

Giving a paper

That it might please you to give quiet pass
Through your dominions for this enterprise,
On such regards of safety and allowance
As therein are set down.

KING CLAUDIUS	It likes us well; And at our more consider'd time well read, Answer, and think upon this business. Meantime we thank you for your well-took labour.

Exeunt VOLTIMAND and CORNELIUS

LORD POLONIUS   This business is well ended.
My liege, since brevity is the soul of wit,
I will be brief: your noble son is mad:
That he is mad, 'tis true: 'tis true 'tis pity;
And pity 'tis 'tis true. Mad let us grant him, then:
And now remains that we find out the cause of this effect,
Or rather say, the cause of this defect,
For this effect defective comes by cause:
Thus it remains, and the remainder thus. Perpend.
I have a daughter who, in her duty and obedience, mark,
Hath given me this: now gather, and surmise.
[Reads] 'To the celestial and my soul's idol, the most
beautified Ophelia,
Doubt thou the stars are fire;
Doubt that the sun doth move;
Doubt truth to be a liar;
But never doubt I love.
'O dear Ophelia, I am ill at these numbers;
I have not art to reckon my groans: but that
I love thee best, O most best, believe it. Adieu.
'Thine evermore most dear lady, whilst
this machine is to him, Hamlet.'
This, in obedience, hath my daughter shown me,
And more above, hath his solicitings,
As they fell out by time, by means and place,
All given to mine ear.

KING CLAUDIUS   But how hath she received his love?

LORD POLONIUS   When I had seen this hot love on the wing
I went round to work,
And my young mistress thus I did bespeak:
'Lord Hamlet is a prince, out of thy star;
This must not be:' and then I precepts gave her,
That she should lock herself from his resort,
Admit no messengers, receive no tokens.
Which done, she took the fruits of my advice;
And he, repulsed, a short tale to make,
Fell into a sadness, then into a fast,

Thence to a watch, thence into a weakness,
Thence to a lightness, and, by this declension,
Into the madness wherein now he raves,
And all we mourn for.

KING CLAUDIUS   Do you think 'tis this?

QUEEN GERTRUDE   It may be, very likely.

LORD POLONIUS   Hath there been such a time
That I have positively said 'Tis so,'
When it proved otherwise?

KING CLAUDIUS   Not that I know.

LORD POLONIUS   *[Pointing to his head and shoulder]*
Take this from this, if this be otherwise:
If circumstances lead me, I will find
Where truth is hid, though it were hid indeed
Within the centre.

KING CLAUDIUS   How may we try it further?

LORD POLONIUS   You know, sometimes he walks four hours together
Here in the lobby.

QUEEN GERTRUDE   So he does indeed.

LORD POLONIUS   At such a time I'll loose my daughter to him:
Be you and I behind an arras then;
Mark the encounter: if he love her not
And be not from his reason fall'n thereon,
Let me be no assistant for a state,
But keep a farm and carters.

KING CLAUDIUS   We will try it.

QUEEN GERTRUDE   But, look, where sadly the poor wretch comes reading.

LORD POLONIUS   Away, I do beseech you, both away:
I'll board him presently.

Exeunt KING CLAUDIUS, QUEEN GERTRUDE, and Attendants. Enter HAMLET, reading

	How does my good Lord Hamlet? Do you know me, my lord?
HAMLET	Excellent well; you are a fishmonger.
LORD POLONIUS	Not I, my lord.
HAMLET	Then I would you were so honest a man.
LORD POLONIUS	Honest, my lord!
HAMLET	Ay, sir; to be honest, as this world goes, is to be one man picked out of ten thousand.
LORD POLONIUS	That's very true, my lord.
HAMLET	For if the sun breed maggots in a dead dog, being a god kissing carrion,--Have you a daughter?
LORD POLONIUS	I have, my lord.
HAMLET	Let her not walk i' the sun: conception is a blessing: but not as your daughter may conceive. Friend, look to 't.
LORD POLONIUS	[Aside] How say you by that? Still harping on my daughter: yet he knew me not at first; he said I was a fishmonger: he is far gone, far gone: I'll speak to him again. What do you read, my lord?
HAMLET	Words, words, words.
LORD POLONIUS	What is the matter, my lord?
HAMLET	Between who?
LORD POLONIUS	I mean, the matter that you read, my lord.
HAMLET	Slanders, sir: for the satirical rogue says here that old men have grey beards, that their faces are wrinkled, their eyes purging thick amber and plum-tree gum and that they have a plentiful lack of wit, together with most weak hams: all which, sir,

though I most powerfully and potently believe, yet
I hold it not honesty to have it thus set down, for
yourself, sir, should be old as I am, if like a crab
you could go backward.

LORD POLONIUS   [Aside] Though this be madness, yet there is method
in 't. Will you walk out of the air, my lord?

HAMLET   Into my grave.

LORD POLONIUS   Indeed, that is out o' the air.
[Aside] How pregnant sometimes his replies are! a happiness
that often madness hits on. I will
leave him, and suddenly contrive the means of
meeting between him and my daughter.--My honourable
lord, I will most humbly take my leave of you.

HAMLET   You cannot, sir, take from me any thing that I will
more willingly part withal: except my life, except
my life, except my life.

LORD POLONIUS   Fare you well, my lord.

Exit POLONIUS

HAMLET   These tedious old fools!

Enter ROSENCRANTZ and GUILDENSTERN

GUILDENSTERN   My honoured lord!

ROSENCRANTZ   My most dear lord!

HAMLET   My excellent good friends! How dost thou,
Guildenstern? Ah, Rosencrantz! Good lads, how do ye both?
What's the news?

ROSENCRANTZ   None, my lord, but that the world's grown honest.

HAMLET   Then is doomsday near: but your news is not true.
Let me question more in particular: what have you,
my good friends, deserved at the hands of fortune,
that she sends you to prison hither?

GUILDENSTERN	Prison, my lord!
HAMLET	Denmark's a prison.
ROSENCRANTZ	Then is the world one.
HAMLET	A goodly one; in which there are many confines, wards and dungeons, Denmark being one o' the worst.
ROSENCRANTZ	We think not so, my lord.
HAMLET	Why, then, 'tis none to you; for there is nothing either good or bad, but thinking makes it so: to me it is a prison.
ROSENCRANTZ	Why then, your ambition makes it one; 'tis too narrow for your mind.
HAMLET	O God, I could be bounded in a nut shell and count myself a king of infinite space, were it not that I have bad dreams. Shall we to the court? for, by my fay, I cannot reason. But, in the beaten way of friendship, what make you at Elsinore?
ROSENCRANTZ	To visit you, my lord; no other occasion.
HAMLET	Were you not sent for?
ROSENCRANTZ	To what end, my lord?
HAMLET	That you must teach me. But let me conjure you, whether you were sent for, or no?
ROSENCRANTZ	[Aside to GUILDENSTERN] What say you?
HAMLET	[Aside] Nay, then, I have an eye of you.--If you love me, hold not off.
GUILDENSTERN	My lord, we were sent for.
HAMLET	I will tell you why; I have of late, but wherefore I know not, lost all my mirth, forgone all custom of exercises; and indeed it goes so heavily

with my disposition that this goodly frame, the earth, seems to me a sterile promontory, this most excellent canopy, the air, look you, this brave o'erhanging firmament, this majestical roof fretted with golden fire, why, it appears no other thing to me than a foul and pestilent congregation of vapours. What a piece of work is a man! how noble in reason! how infinite in faculty! in form and moving how express and admirable! in action how like an angel! in apprehension how like a god! the beauty of the world! the paragon of animals! And yet, to me, what is this quintessence of dust? man delights not me: no, nor woman neither, though by your smiling you seem to say so.

ROSENCRANTZ   My lord, if you delight not in man, what lenten entertainment the players shall receive from you: hither are they coming, to offer you service.

HAMLET   He that plays the king shall be welcome; his majesty shall have tribute of me.

Flourish of trumpets within

GUILDENSTERN   There are the players.

HAMLET   Gentlemen, you are welcome to Elsinore.

Enter POLONIUS

LORD POLONIUS   Well be with you, gentlemen!

HAMLET   I will prophesy he comes to tell me of the players; mark it.

LORD POLONIUS   My lord, I have news to tell you.

HAMLET   My lord, I have news to tell you.

LORD POLONIUS   The actors are come hither, my lord.
The best actors in the world, either for tragedy,
comedy, history, pastoral, pastoral-comical,

historical-pastoral, tragical-historical, tragical-comical-historical-pastoral, scene individable, or poem unlimited.

HAMLET	O Jephthah, judge of Israel, what a treasure hadst thou!
LORD POLONIUS	What a treasure had he, my lord?
HAMLET	Why, 'One fair daughter and no more, The which he loved passing well.'
LORD POLONIUS	[Aside] Still on my daughter.

Enter four or five Players

You are welcome, masters; welcome, all. I am glad to see thee well. Welcome, good friends.

HAMLET	Good my lord, will you see the players well bestowed? Do you hear, let them be well used.
LORD POLONIUS	My lord, I will use them according to their desert.
HAMLET	God's bodykins, man, much better: use every man after his desert, and who should 'scape whipping? Use them after your own honour and dignity: the less they deserve, the more merit is in your bounty. Take them in.
LORD POLONIUS	Come, sirs.
HAMLET	Follow him, friends: we'll hear a play to-morrow.

Exit POLONIUS with all the Players but the First

Dost thou hear me, old friend; can you play the Murder of Gonzago?

First Player	Ay, my lord.
HAMLET	We'll ha't to-morrow night. You could, for a need, study a speech of some dozen or sixteen lines, which I would set down and insert in't, could you not?

First Player	Ay, my lord.
HAMLET	Very well. Follow that lord; and look you mock him not.

Exit First Player

My good friends, I'll leave you till night: you are
welcome to Elsinore.

ROSENCRANTZ	Good my lord!
HAMLET	Ay, so, God be wi' ye;

Exeunt ROSENCRANTZ and GUILDENSTERN

Now I am alone.
O, what a rogue and peasant slave am I!
Is it not monstrous that this player here,
But in a fiction, in a dream of passion,
Could force his soul so to his own conceit
That from her working all his visage wann'd,
Tears in his eyes, distraction in's aspect,
A broken voice, and his whole function suiting
With forms to his conceit? and all for nothing!
For Hecuba!
What's Hecuba to him, or he to Hecuba,
That he should weep for her? What would he do,
Had he the motive and the cue for passion
That I have? He would drown the stage with tears
And cleave the general ear with horrid speech,
Make mad the guilty and appal the free,
Confound the ignorant, and amaze indeed
The very faculties of eyes and ears. Yet I,
A dull and muddy-mettled rascal, peak,
Like John-a-dreams, unpregnant of my cause,
And can say nothing; no, not for a king,
Upon whose property and most dear life
A damn'd defeat was made. Am I a coward?
Who calls me villain? breaks my pate across?
Plucks off my beard, and blows it in my face?

Tweaks me by the nose? gives me the lie i' the throat,
As deep as to the lungs? who does me this?
Ha!
'Swounds, I should take it: for it cannot be
But I am pigeon-liver'd and lack gall
To make oppression bitter, or ere this
I should have fatted all the region kites
With this slave's offal: bloody, bawdy villain!
Remorseless, treacherous, lecherous, kindless villain!
O, vengeance!
Why, what an ass am I! This is most brave,
That I, the son of a dear father murder'd,
Prompted to my revenge by heaven and hell,
Must, like a whore, unpack my heart with words,
And fall a-cursing, like a very drab,
A scullion!
Fie upon't! foh! About, my brain! I have heard
That guilty creatures sitting at a play
Have by the very cunning of the scene
Been struck so to the soul that presently
They have proclaim'd their malefactions;
For murder, though it have no tongue, will speak
With most miraculous organ. I'll have these players
Play something like the murder of my father
Before mine uncle: I'll observe his looks;
I'll tent him to the quick: if he but blench,
I know my course. The spirit that I have seen
May be the devil: and the devil hath power
To assume a pleasing shape; yea, and perhaps
Out of my weakness and my melancholy,
As he is very potent with such spirits,
Abuses me to damn me: I'll have grounds
More relative than this: the play 's the thing
Wherein I'll catch the conscience of the king.

Exit

35

ACT III

Act III Scene I

A room in the castle.

Enter KING CLAUDIUS, QUEEN GERTRUDE, POLONIUS, OPHELIA

KING CLAUDIUS   Sweet Gertrude, we have closely sent for Hamlet hither,
That he, as 'twere by accident, may here
Affront Ophelia: her father and myself, lawful espials,
Will so bestow ourselves that, seeing, unseen,
We may of their encounter frankly judge,
And gather by him, as he is behaved,
If 't be the affliction of his love or no
That thus he suffers for.

QUEEN GERTRUDE   For your part, Ophelia, I do wish
That your good beauties be the happy cause
Of Hamlet's wildness: so shall I hope your virtues
Will bring him to his wonted way again,
To both your honours.

OPHELIA   Madam, I wish it may.

Exit QUEEN GERTRUDE

LORD POLONIUS   Ophelia, read on this book;
That show of such an exercise may colour
Your loneliness. We are oft to blame in this,--
'Tis too much proved--that with devotion's visage
And pious action we do sugar o'er
The devil himself.

KING CLAUDIUS   [Aside] O, 'tis too true!
How smart a lash that speech doth give my conscience!
The harlot's cheek, beautied with plastering art,
Is not more ugly to the thing that helps it
Than is my deed to my most painted word:
O heavy burthen!

LORD POLONIUS   I hear him coming: let's withdraw, my lord.

Exeunt KING CLAUDIUS and POLONIUS. Enter HAMLET

HAMLET   To be, or not to be: that is the question:
Whether 'tis nobler in the mind to suffer
The slings and arrows of outrageous fortune,
Or to take arms against a sea of troubles,
And by opposing end them? To die: to sleep;
No more; and by a sleep to say we end
The heart-ache and the thousand natural shocks
That flesh is heir to, 'tis a consummation
Devoutly to be wish'd. To die, to sleep;
To sleep: perchance to dream: ay, there's the rub;
For in that sleep of death what dreams may come
When we have shuffled off this mortal coil,
Must give us pause: there's the respect
That makes calamity of so long life;
For who would bear the whips and scorns of time,
The oppressor's wrong, the proud man's contumely,
The pangs of despised love, the law's delay,
The insolence of office and the spurns
That patient merit of the unworthy takes,
When he himself might his quietus make
With a bare bodkin? who would fardels bear,
To grunt and sweat under a weary life,
But that the dread of something after death,
The undiscover'd country from whose bourn
No traveller returns, puzzles the will
And makes us rather bear those ills we have
Than fly to others that we know not of?
Thus conscience does make cowards of us all;
And thus the native hue of resolution
Is sicklied o'er with the pale cast of thought,
And enterprises of great pith and moment
With this regard their currents turn awry,
And lose the name of action.--Soft you now!
The fair Ophelia! Nymph, in thy orisons
Be all my sins remember'd.

OPHELIA	Good my lord, How does your honour for this many a day?
HAMLET	I humbly thank you; well, well, well.
OPHELIA	My lord, I have remembrances of yours, That I have longed long to re-deliver; I pray you, now receive them.
HAMLET	No, not I; I never gave you aught.
OPHELIA	My honour'd lord, you know right well you did; And, with them, words of so sweet breath composed As made the things more rich: their perfume lost, Take these again; for to the noble mind Rich gifts wax poor when givers prove unkind. There, my lord.
HAMLET	Ha, ha! are you honest? I did love you once.
OPHELIA	Indeed, my lord, you made me believe so.
HAMLET	You should not have believed me; I loved you not.
OPHELIA	I was the more deceived.
HAMLET	Get thee to a nunnery: why wouldst thou be a breeder of sinners? I am myself indifferent honest; but yet I could accuse me of such things that it were better my mother had not borne me: I am very proud, revengeful, ambitious, with more offences at my beck than I have thoughts to put them in, imagination to give them shape, or time to act them in. What should such fellows as I do crawling between earth and heaven? We are arrant knaves, all; believe none of us. Go thy ways to a nunnery. Where's your father?
OPHELIA	At home, my lord.
HAMLET	Let the doors be shut upon him, that he may play the fool no where but in's own house. Farewell.

OPHELIA	O, help him, you sweet heavens!
HAMLET	If thou dost marry, I'll give thee this plague for thy dowry: be thou as chaste as ice, as pure as snow, thou shalt not escape calumny. Get thee to a nunnery, go: farewell. Or, if thou wilt needs marry, marry a fool; for wise men know well enough what monsters you make of them. To a nunnery, go, and quickly too. Farewell.
OPHELIA	O heavenly powers, restore him!
HAMLET	I have heard of your paintings too, well enough; God has given you one face, and you make yourselves another: you jig, you amble, and you lisp, and nick-name God's creatures, and make your wantonness your ignorance. Go to, I'll no more on't; it hath made me mad. I say, we will have no more marriages: those that are married already, all but one, shall live; the rest shall keep as they are. To a nunnery, go.

Exit

OPHELIA	O, what a noble mind is here o'erthrown! O, woe is me, to have seen what I have seen, See what I see!

Re-enter KING CLAUDIUS and POLONIUS

KING CLAUDIUS	Love! his affections do not that way tend; Nor what he spake, though it lack'd form a little, Was not like madness. There's something in his soul, O'er which his melancholy sits on brood; And I do doubt the hatch and the disclose Will be some danger: which for to prevent, I have in quick determination Thus set it down: he shall with speed to England, For the demand of our neglected tribute Haply the seas and countries different With variable objects shall expel This something-settled matter in his heart,

Whereon his brains still beating puts him thus
From fashion of himself. What think you on't?

LORD POLONIUS   It shall do well: but yet do I believe
The origin and commencement of his grief
Sprung from neglected love.
But, if you hold it fit, after the play
Let his queen mother all alone entreat him
To show his grief: let her be round with him;
And I'll be placed, so please you, in the ear
Of all their conference. If she find him not,
To England send him, or confine him where
Your wisdom best shall think.

KING CLAUDIUS   It shall be so:
Madness in great ones must not unwatch'd go.

Exeunt

Act III Scene II

A hall in the castle.

Enter HAMLET and HORATIO

HORATIO
Here, sweet lord, at your service.

HAMLET
Horatio, thou art e'en as just a man
As e'er my conversation coped withal.
There is a play to-night before the king;
One scene of it comes near the circumstance
Which I have told thee of my father's death:
I prithee, when thou seest that act afoot,
Even with the very comment of thy soul
Observe mine uncle: if his occulted guilt
Do not itself unkennel in one speech,
It is a damned ghost that we have seen,
And my imaginations are as foul
As Vulcan's stithy. Give him heedful note;
For I mine eyes will rivet to his face,
And after we will both our judgments join
In censure of his seeming.

HORATIO
Well, my lord:
If he steal aught the whilst this play is playing,
And 'scape detecting, I will pay the theft.

HAMLET
They are coming to the play; I must be idle:
Get you a place.

Danish march. A flourish. Enter KING CLAUDIUS, QUEEN GERTRUDE, POLONIUS, OPHELIA, ROZENCRANTZ and GILDENSTERN

HAMLET
Be the players ready?

ROSENCRANTZ
Ay, my lord; they stay upon your patience.

QUEEN GERTRUDE
Come hither, my dear Hamlet, sit by me.

HAMLET
No, good mother, here's metal more attractive.

LORD POLONIUS	[To KING CLAUDIUS] O, ho! do you mark that?
HAMLET	Lady, shall I lie in your lap?
OPHELIA	No, my lord.
HAMLET	I mean, my head upon your lap?
OPHELIA	Ay, my lord.
HAMLET	Do you think I meant country matters?
OPHELIA	I think nothing, my lord.
HAMLET	That's a fair thought to lie between maids' legs.
OPHELIA	What is, my lord?
HAMLET	Nothing.
OPHELIA	You are merry, my lord.
HAMLET	Who, I?
OPHELIA	Ay, my lord.
HAMLET	O God, your only jig-maker. What should a man do but be merry? for, look you, how cheerfully my mother looks, and my father died within these two hours.
OPHELIA	Nay, 'tis twice two months, my lord.
HAMLET	So long? O heavens! die two months ago, and not forgotten yet? Then there's hope a great man's memory may outlive his life half a year.

Hautboys play. The dumb-show enters

Enter a King and a Queen very lovingly; the Queen embracing him, and he her. She kneels, and makes show of protestation unto him. He takes her up, and declines his head upon her neck: lays him down upon a bank of flowers: she, seeing him asleep, leaves him. Anon comes in a fellow, takes off his crown, kisses it, and pours poison in the King's ears, and exit. The Queen returns; finds the King dead, and makes passionate action. The Poisoner, with some two or three Mutes, comes in again, seeming to lament with her. The dead body is carried away. The Poisoner wooes the Queen with gifts: she seems loath and unwilling awhile, but in the end accepts his love

Exeunt

OPHELIA	What means this, my lord?
HAMLET	Marry, this is mischief.
OPHELIA	Belike this show imports the argument of the play.

Enter Prologue

HAMLET	We shall know by this fellow: the players cannot keep counsel; they'll tell all.
Prologue	For us, and for our tragedy, Here stooping to your clemency, We beg your hearing patiently.

Exit

OPHELIA	'Tis brief, my lord.
HAMLET	As woman's love.

Enter two Players, King and Queen

Player King	Full thirty times hath Phoebus' cart gone round Neptune's salt wash and Tellus' orbed ground, Since love our hearts and Hymen did our hands Unite commutual in most sacred bands.
Player Queen	So many journeys may the sun and moon Make us again count o'er ere love be done! But, woe is me, you are so sick of late.
Player King	'Faith, I must leave thee, love, and shortly too; My operant powers their functions leave to do: And thou shalt live in this fair world behind, Honour'd, beloved; and haply one as kind For husband shalt thou--

Player Queen	O, confound the rest! Such love must needs be treason in my breast: In second husband let me be accurst! None wed the second but who kill'd the first. A second time I kill my husband dead, When second husband kisses me in bed.
Player King	I do believe you think what now you speak; But what we do determine oft we break. So think thou wilt no second husband wed; But die thy thoughts when thy first lord is dead.
Player Queen	Both here and hence pursue me lasting strife, If, once a widow, ever I be wife!
HAMLET	If she should break it now!
Player King	'Tis deeply sworn. Sweet, leave me here awhile; My spirits grow dull, and fain I would beguile The tedious day with sleep.

Sleeps - Exit Player Queen

HAMLET	Madam, how like you this play?
QUEEN GERTRUDE	The lady protests too much, methinks.
HAMLET	O, but she'll keep her word.
KING CLAUDIUS	Have you heard the argument? Is there no offence in 't?
HAMLET	No, no, they do but jest, poison in jest; no offence i' the world.
KING CLAUDIUS	What do you call the play?
HAMLET	The Mouse-trap. This play is the image of a murder done in Vienna: 'tis a knavish piece of work: but what o' that? your majesty and we that have free souls, it touches us not: let the galled jade wince, our withers are unwrung.

Enter LUCIANUS

This is one Lucianus, nephew to the king.

LUCIANUS	Thoughts black, hands apt, drugs fit, and time agreeing; Confederate season, else no creature seeing; Thou mixture rank, thy natural magic and dire property, On wholesome life usurp immediately.

Pours the poison into the sleeper's ears

HAMLET	He poisons him i' the garden for's estate, you shall see anon how the murderer gets the love of Gonzago's wife.
OPHELIA	The king rises.
HAMLET	What, frighted with false fire!
KING CLAUDIUS	Give me some light: away!
All	Lights, lights, lights!

Exeunt all but HAMLET and HORATIO

HAMLET	O good Horatio, I'll take the ghost's word for a thousand pound. Didst perceive?
HORATIO	Very well, my lord.
HAMLET	Upon the talk of the poisoning?
HORATIO	I did very well note him.
HAMLET	Ah, ha! Come, some music! come, the recorders! For if the king like not the comedy, Why then, belike, he likes it not, perdy. Come, some music!

Re-enter ROSENCRANTZ and GUILDENSTERN

GUILDENSTERN	Good my lord, vouchsafe me a word with you. The king, sir, is in his retirement marvellous distempered. The queen, your mother, in most great affliction of Spirit, hath sent me to you.
ROSENCRANTZ	She says; your behaviour hath struck her Into amazement and admiration.

	She desires to speak with you in her closet, Ere you go to bed.
HAMLET	We shall obey, were she ten times our mother. Have you any further trade with us?
ROSENCRANTZ	Good my lord, what is your cause of distemper? you do, surely, bar the door upon your own liberty, if you deny your griefs to our friend.
HAMLET	Sir, I lack advancement.
ROSENCRANTZ	How can that be, when you have the voice of the king himself for your succession in Denmark?

Re-enter Players with recorders

HAMLET	O, the recorders! let me see one. To withdraw with you:--why do you go about to recover the wind of me, as if you would drive me into a toil?
GUILDENSTERN	O, my lord, if my duty be too bold, my love is too unmannerly.
HAMLET	I do not well understand that. Will you play upon this pipe?
GUILDENSTERN	My lord, I cannot.
HAMLET	I pray you.
GUILDENSTERN	Believe me, I cannot. I know no touch of it, my lord.
HAMLET	'Tis as easy as lying: govern these ventages with your fingers and thumb, give it breath with your mouth, and it will discourse most eloquent music. Look you, these are the stops.
GUILDENSTERN	But these cannot I command to any utterance of harmony; I have not the skill.
HAMLET	Why, look you now, how unworthy a thing you make of me! You would play upon me; you would seem to know

my stops; you would pluck out the heart of my
mystery; you would sound me from my lowest note to
the top of my compass: and there is much music,
excellent voice, in this little organ; yet cannot
you make it speak. 'Sblood, do you think I am
easier to be played on than a pipe?

Enter POLONIUS

God bless you, sir!

LORD POLONIUS   My lord, the queen would speak with you, and
presently.

HAMLET   Then I will come to my mother by and by. They fool
me to the top of my bent. I will come by and by.

Exit POLONIUS

Leave me, friends.

Exeunt all but HAMLET

Now could I drink hot blood,
And do such bitter business as the day
Would quake to look on. Soft! now to my mother.
O heart, lose not thy nature; let not ever
The soul of Nero enter this firm bosom:
Let me be cruel, not unnatural:
I will speak daggers to her, but use none;
My tongue and soul in this be hypocrites;
How in my words soever she be shent,
To give them seals never, my soul, consent!

Exit

Act III Scene III

A room in the castle.

Enter KING CLAUDIUS, ROSENCRANTZ, and GUILDENSTERN

KING CLAUDIUS I like him not, nor stands it safe with us
To let his madness range. Therefore prepare you;
I your commission will forthwith dispatch,
And he to England shall along with you:
The terms of our estate may not endure
Hazard so dangerous as doth hourly grow
Out of his lunacies.

GUILDENSTERN We will ourselves provide:
Most holy and religious fear it is
To keep those many many bodies safe
That live and feed upon your majesty.

KING CLAUDIUS Arm you, I pray you, to this speedy voyage;
For we will fetters put upon this fear,
Which now goes too free-footed.

ROS & GUILD We will haste us.

Exeunt ROSENCRANTZ and GUILDENSTERN. Enter POLONIUS

LORD POLONIUS My lord, he's going to his mother's closet:
Behind the arras I'll convey myself,
To hear the process. Fare you well, my liege:
I'll call upon you ere you go to bed,
And tell you what I know.

KING CLAUDIUS Thanks, dear my lord.

Exit POLONIUS

O, my offence is rank it smells to heaven;
It hath the primal eldest curse upon't,
A brother's murder. Pray can I not,
Though inclination be as sharp as will:

My stronger guilt defeats my strong intent;
But, O, what form of prayer
Can serve my turn? 'Forgive me my foul murder'?
That cannot be; since I am still possess'd
Of those effects for which I did the murder,
My crown, mine own ambition and my queen.
May one be pardon'd and retain the offence?
Try what repentance can: what can it not?
Yet what can it when one can not repent?
Bow, stubborn knees; and, heart with strings of steel,
Be soft as sinews of the newborn babe!
All may be well.

Retires and kneels. Enter HAMLET

HAMLET   Now might I do it pat, now he is praying;
And now I'll do't. And so he goes to heaven;
And so am I revenged. That would be scann'd:
A villain kills my father; and for that,
I, his sole son, do this same villain send
To heaven. And am I then revenged,
To take him in the purging of his soul,
When he is fit and season'd for his passage?
No!
Up, sword; and know thou a more horrid hent:
When he is drunk asleep, or in his rage,
Or in the incestuous pleasure of his bed;
At gaming, swearing, or about some act
That has no relish of salvation in't;
Then trip him, that his heels may kick at heaven,
And that his soul may be as damn'd and black
As hell, whereto it goes. My mother stays:
This physic but prolongs thy sickly days.

Exit

KING CLAUDIUS   [Rising] My words fly up, my thoughts remain below:
Words without thoughts never to heaven go.

Exit

Act III Scene IV

The Queen's closet.

Enter QUEEN GERTRUDE and POLONIUS

LORD POLONIUS   Tell him his pranks have been too broad to bear with,
And that your grace hath screen'd and stood between
Much heat and him. I'll sconce me even here.

QUEEN GERTRUDE   Fear me not: withdraw, I hear him coming.

POLONIUS hides behind the arras. Enter HAMLET

HAMLET   Now, mother, what's the matter?

QUEEN GERTRUDE   Hamlet, thou hast thy father much offended.

HAMLET   Mother, you have my father much offended.

QUEEN GERTRUDE   Come, come, you answer with an idle tongue.

HAMLET   Go, go, you question with a wicked tongue.

QUEEN GERTRUDE   Why, how now, Hamlet! Have you forgot me?

HAMLET   No, you are the queen, your husband's brother's wife;
And, would it were not so, you are my mother.

QUEEN GERTRUDE   Nay, then, I'll set those to you that can speak.

HAMLET   Come, come, and sit you down; you shall not budge;
You go not till I set you up a glass
Where you may see the inmost part of you.

QUEEN GERTRUDE   What wilt thou do? thou wilt not murder me?
Help, help, ho!

LORD POLONIUS   *[Behind]* What, ho! help, help, help!

HAMLET   *[Drawing]* How now! a rat? Dead, for a ducat, dead!

Makes a pass through the arras

LORD POLONIUS	*[Behind]* O, I am slain!

Falls and dies

QUEEN GERTRUDE	O me, what hast thou done?
HAMLET	Nay, I know not: Is it the king?
QUEEN GERTRUDE	O, what a rash and bloody deed is this!
HAMLET	A bloody deed! almost as bad, good mother, As kill a king, and marry with his brother.
QUEEN GERTRUDE	As kill a king!
HAMLET	Ay, lady, 'twas my word.

Lifts up the array and discovers POLONIUS

	Thou wretched, rash, intruding fool, farewell! I took thee for thy better.
QUEEN GERTRUDE	What have I done, that thou darest wag thy tongue In noise so rude against me?
HAMLET	Such an act That blurs the grace and blush of modesty, Calls virtue hypocrite, and makes marriage-vows As false as dicers' oaths.
QUEEN GERTRUDE	Ay me, what act?
HAMLET	Look here, upon this picture, and on this, The counterfeit presentment of two brothers. See, what a grace was seated on this brow: This was your husband. Look you now, what follows: Here is your husband; like a mildew'd ear, Blasting his wholesome brother. What judgment Would step from this to this? O shame! where is thy blush?

QUEEN GERTRUDE	O Hamlet, speak no more: Thou turn'st mine eyes into my very soul.
HAMLET	Nay, but to live In the rank sweat of an enseamed bed, Stew'd in corruption, honeying and making love Over the nasty sty,--
QUEEN GERTRUDE	O, speak to me no more; These words, like daggers, enter in mine ears; No more, sweet Hamlet!
HAMLET	A murderer and a villain; A slave, a vice of kings; A cutpurse of the empire and the rule, That from a shelf the precious diadem stole, And put it in his pocket!
QUEEN GERTRUDE	No more!
HAMLET	A king of shreds and patches,--

Enter Ghost

	Save me, you heavenly guards! What would your gracious figure?
QUEEN GERTRUDE	Alas, he's mad!
HAMLET	Do you not come your tardy son to chide? O, say!
Ghost	Do not forget: this visitation Is but to whet thy almost blunted purpose.
QUEEN GERTRUDE	Alas, how is't with you, That you do bend your eye on vacancy And with the incorporal air do hold discourse? O gentle son, whereon do you look?
HAMLET	On him, on him! Look you, how pale he glares! Do you see nothing there?
QUEEN GERTRUDE	Nothing at all; yet all that is I see.

HAMLET   Why, look you there! look, how it steals away!
My father, in his habit as he lived!
Look, where he goes, even now, out at the portal!

Exit Ghost

QUEEN GERTRUDE   This the very coinage of your brain.

HAMLET   It is not madness
That I have utter'd: Mother, for love of grace,
Confess yourself to heaven;
Repent what's past; avoid what is to come;
And do not spread the compost on the weeds,
To make them ranker.

QUEEN GERTRUDE   O Hamlet, thou hast cleft my heart in twain.

HAMLET   O, throw away the worser part of it,
And live the purer with the other half.
Good night: but go not to mine uncle's bed;
For this same lord,

Pointing to POLONIUS

I do repent: I will bestow him, and will answer well
The death I gave him. So, again, good night.
One word more, good lady.

QUEEN GERTRUDE   What shall I do?

HAMLET   I must to England; you know that?
There's letters seal'd: and my two schoolfellows,
Whom I will trust as I will adders fang'd,
They bear the mandate; they must sweep my way,
And marshal me to knavery. Let it work;
For 'tis the sport to have the engineer
Hoist with his own petard: and 't shall go hard
But I will delve one yard below their mines,
And blow them at the moon: O, 'tis most sweet,
When in one line two crafts directly meet.
This man shall set me packing:

I'll lug the guts into the neighbour room.
Mother, good night.

Exeunt severally; HAMLET dragging in POLONIUS

ACT IV

Act IV Scene I

A room in the castle.

Enter KING CLAUDIUS, QUEEN GERTRUDE,

KING CLAUDIUS   Where is your son?

QUEEN GERTRUDE   Mad as the sea and wind, when both contend
Which is the mightier: in his lawless fit,
Behind the arras hearing something stir,
Whips out his rapier, cries, 'A rat, a rat!'
And, in this brainish apprehension, kills
The unseen good old man.

KING CLAUDIUS   O heavy deed!
It had been so with us, had we been there:
His liberty is full of threats to all;
Alas, how shall this bloody deed be answer'd?
It will be laid to us, whose providence
Should have restrain'd this mad young man.
Where is he gone?

QUEEN GERTRUDE   To draw apart the body he hath kill'd.

KING CLAUDIUS   O Gertrude, we will ship him hence: and this vile deed
We must, with all our majesty and skill,
Both countenance and excuse. Ho, Guildenstern!

Enter ROSENCRANTZ and GUILDENSTERN

Friends both, Hamlet in madness hath Polonius slain,
And from his mother's closet hath he dragg'd him:
Go seek him out; speak fair, and bring the body
Into the chapel. I pray you, haste in this.

Exeunt ROSENCRANTZ and GUILDENSTERN

Come, come away!
My soul is full of discord and dismay.

Exeunt

Act IV Scene II

Another room in the castle.

Enter HAMLET

HAMLET   Safely stowed.

GUIDENSTERN   *[Within]* Hamlet! Lord Hamlet!

Enter ROSENCRANTZ and GUILDENSTERN

ROSENCRANTZ   My lord, you must tell us where the body is, and go
                    with us to the king.

HAMLET   The body is with the king, but the king is not with
                    the body. The king is a thing--

GUILDENSTERN   A thing, my lord!

HAMLET   Of nothing: bring me to him. Hide fox, and all after.

Exeunt

Act IV Scene III

Another room in the castle.

Enter KING CLAUDIUS, attended

KING CLAUDIUS   I have sent to seek him, and to find the body.
How dangerous is it that this man goes loose!
Yet must not we put the strong law on him:
He's loved of the distracted multitude,
This sudden sending him away must seem
Deliberate pause:

Enter ROSENCRANTZ

ROSENCRANTZ   Where the dead body is bestow'd, my lord,
We cannot get from him.

KING CLAUDIUS   But where is he?

ROSENCRANTZ   Without, my lord; guarded, to know your pleasure.

KING CLAUDIUS   Bring him before us.

Enter HAMLET and GUILDENSTERN

KING CLAUDIUS   Now, Hamlet, where's Polonius?

HAMLET   At supper.

KING CLAUDIUS   At supper! where?

HAMLET   Not where he eats, but where he is eaten: a certain
convocation of politic worms are e'en at him.
A man may fish with the worm that hath eat of a king.

KING CLAUDIUS   Where is Polonius?

HAMLET   In heaven; send hither to see: if your messenger
find him not there, seek him i' the other place
yourself. But indeed, if you find him not within
this month, you shall nose him as you go up the
stairs into the lobby.

KING CLAUDIUS	*[To some Attendants]* Go seek him there.
HAMLET	He will stay till ye come.

Exeunt Attendants

KING CLAUDIUS	Hamlet, this deed, for thine especial safety,-- Which we do tender, as we dearly grieve For that which thou hast done,--must send thee hence With fiery quickness: therefore prepare thyself; The bark is ready, and the wind at help, The associates tend, and every thing is bent For England.
HAMLET	For England! Farewell, dear mother.
KING CLAUDIUS	Thy loving father, Hamlet.
HAMLET	My mother: father and mother is man and wife; man and wife is one flesh; and so, my mother. Come, for England!

Exeunt HAMLET, ROSENCRANTZ and GUILDENSTERN

KING CLAUDIUS	And, England, if my love thou hold'st at aught-- thou mayst not coldly set Our sovereign process; which imports at full, By letters congruing to that effect, The present death of Hamlet. Do it, England.

Exit

Act IV Scene IV

A plain in Denmark.

Enter FORTINBRAS, a Captain, and Soldiers, marching

PRINCE FORTINBRAS   Go, captain, from me greet the Danish king;
Tell him that, by his licence, Fortinbras
Craves the conveyance of a promised march
Over his kingdom.

Captain   I will do't, my lord.

Enter HAMLET, ROSENCRANTZ, GUILDENSTERN, and others

HAMLET   Good sir, whose powers are these?

Captain   They are of Norway, sir.

HAMLET   How purposed, sir, I pray you?

Captain   Against some part of Poland.

HAMLET   Who commands them, sir?

Captain   The nephews to old Norway, Fortinbras.

HAMLET   Goes it against the main of Poland, sir,
Or for some frontier?

Captain   Truly to speak, and with no addition,
We go to gain a little patch of ground
That hath in it no profit but the name.
To pay five ducats, five, I would not farm it.

HAMLET   Why, then the Polack never will defend it.

Captain   Yes, it is already garrison'd.
God be wi' you, sir.

Exit

ROSENCRANTZ   Wilt please you go, my lord?

HAMLET   I'll be with you straight go a little before.

Exeunt all except HAMLET

How all occasions do inform against me,
And spur my dull revenge!
Witness this army of such mass and charge
Led by a delicate and tender prince,
Whose spirit with divine ambition puff'd
Makes mouths at the invisible event,
Exposing what is mortal and unsure
To all that fortune, death and danger dare,
Even for an egg-shell. How stand I then,
That have a father kill'd, a mother stain'd,
Excitements of my reason and my blood,
And let all sleep? while, to my shame, I see
The imminent death of twenty thousand men,
That, for a fantasy and trick of fame,
Go to their graves like beds? O, from this time forth,
My thoughts be bloody, or be nothing worth!

Exit

Act IV Scene V

Elsinore. A room in the castle.

Enter QUEEN GERTRUDE, HORATIO, and a Gentleman

QUEEN GERTRUDE	I will not speak with her.
Gentleman	She is importunate, indeed distract: Her mood will needs be pitied. She speaks much of her father; says she hears There's tricks i' the world; and hems, and beats her heart.
HORATIO	'Twere good she were spoken with; for she may strew Dangerous conjectures in ill-breeding minds.
QUEEN GERTRUDE	Let her come in.

Enter OPHELIA

OPHELIA	Where is the beauteous majesty of Denmark?
QUEEN GERTRUDE	How now, Ophelia!
OPHELIA	*[Sings]* He is dead and gone, lady, He is dead and gone; At his head a grass-green turf, At his heels a stone. White his shroud as the mountain snow,--

Enter KING CLAUDIUS

QUEEN GERTRUDE	Alas, look here, my lord.
KING CLAUDIUS	How do you, pretty lady?
OPHELIA	Well, God 'ild you! They say the owl was a baker's daughter. Lord, we know what we are, but know not what we may be. God be at your table!
KING CLAUDIUS	Conceit upon her father.
OPHELIA	*[Sings]* To-morrow is Saint Valentine's day, All in the morning betime,

And I a maid at your window,
To be your Valentine.
Then up he rose, and donn'd his clothes,
And dupp'd the chamber-door;
Let in the maid, that out a maid
Never departed more.

KING CLAUDIUS   Pretty Ophelia!

OPHELIA   Indeed, la, without an oath, I'll make an end on't:

[Sings] By Gis and by Saint Charity,
Alack, and fie for shame!
Young men will do't, if they come to't;
By cock, they are to blame.
Quoth she, before you tumbled me,
You promised me to wed.
So would I ha' done, by yonder sun,
An thou hadst not come to my bed.

KING CLAUDIUS   How long hath she been thus?

OPHELIA   I hope all will be well. We must be patient: but I
cannot choose but weep, to think they should lay him
i' the cold ground. My brother shall know of it:
and so I thank you for your good counsel. Come, my
coach! Good night, ladies; good night, sweet ladies;
good night, good night.

Exit

KING CLAUDIUS   Follow her close; give her good watch,
I pray you.

Exit HORATIO

O, this is the poison of deep grief; it springs
All from her father's death. O Gertrude, Gertrude,
When sorrows come, they come not single spies
But in battalions. First, her father slain:
Next, your son gone; and poor Ophelia
Divided from herself and her fair judgment:
Last, and as much containing as all these,

Her brother is in secret come from France.

A noise within

QUEEN GERTRUDE   Alack, what noise is this?

KING CLAUDIUS   Where are my Switzers? Let them guard the door.

Enter another Gentleman

What is the matter?

Gentleman   Save yourself, my lord:
Young Laertes, in a riotous head,
O'erbears your officers. The rabble call him lord;
They cry 'Choose we: Laertes shall be king:'
Caps, hands, and tongues, applaud it to the clouds:
'Laertes shall be king, Laertes king!'

Noise within. Enter LAERTES, armed

LAERTES   O thou vile king, give me my father!

QUEEN GERTRUDE   Calmly, good Laertes.

LAERTES   That drop of blood that's calm proclaims me bastard.

KING CLAUDIUS   What is the cause, Laertes,
That thy rebellion looks so giant-like?
Let him go, Gertrude; do not fear our person.
Tell me, Laertes,
Why thou art thus incensed. Speak, man.

LAERTES   Where is my father?

KING CLAUDIUS   Dead.

QUEEN GERTRUDE   But not by him.

KING CLAUDIUS   Let him demand his fill.

LAERTES   How came he dead? I'll not be juggled with:
To hell, allegiance! I'll be revenged
Most thoroughly for my father.

KING CLAUDIUS	Good Laertes,
	That I am guiltless of your father's death,
	And am most sensible in grief for it,
	It shall as level to your judgment pierce
	As day does to your eye.

| LAERTES | How now! what noise is that? |

Re-enter OPHELIA

O heat, dry up my brains! tears seven times salt,
Burn out the sense and virtue of mine eye!
By heaven, thy madness shall be paid by weight,
Till our scale turn the beam. O rose of May!
Dear maid, kind sister, sweet Ophelia!
O heavens! is't possible, a young maid's wits
Should be as mortal as an old man's life?

OPHELIA	*[Sings]* They bore him barefaced on the bier;
	Hey non nonny, nonny, hey nonny;
	And in his grave rain'd many a tear:--
	Fare you well, my dove!

| LAERTES | Hadst thou thy wits, and didst persuade revenge, |
| | It could not move thus. |

OPHELIA	There's rosemary, that's for remembrance; pray,
	love, remember: and there is pansies. that's for thoughts.
	There's a daisy: I would give you
	some violets, but they withered all when my father
	died: they say he made a good end,--

[Sings] And will he not come again?
And will he not come again?
No, no, he is dead:
Go to thy death-bed. God be wi' ye.

Exit

| LAERTES | Do you see this, O God? |

| KING CLAUDIUS | Laertes, I must commune with your grief, |
| | Or you deny me right. Go but apart, |

Make choice of whom your wisest friends you will.
And they shall hear and judge 'twixt you and me:
If by direct or by collateral hand
They find us touch'd, we will our kingdom give,
Our crown, our life, and all that we can ours,
To you in satisfaction; but if not,
Be you content to lend your patience to us,
And we shall jointly labour with your soul
To give it due content.

LAERTES
Let this be so;
His means of death, his obscure funeral--
No trophy, sword, nor hatchment o'er his bones,
No noble rite nor formal ostentation--
Cry to be heard, as 'twere from heaven to earth,
That I must call't in question.

KING CLAUDIUS
So you shall;
And where the offence is let the great axe fall.
I pray you, go with me.

Exeunt

Act IV Scene VI

Another room in the castle.

Enter HORATIO and a Servant

HORATIO	What are they that would speak with me?

Servant	Sailors, sir: they say they have letters for you.

HORATIO	Let them come in.
Enter Sailors

First Sailor	God bless you, sir. There's a letter for you, sir; it comes from the ambassador that was bound for England.

HORATIO	*[Reads]* 'Horatio, when thou shalt have overlooked this, give these fellows some means to the king: they have letters for him. Ere we were two days old at sea, a pirate of very warlike appointment gave us chase. Finding ourselves too slow of sail, we put on a compelled valour, and in the grapple I boarded them: on the instant they got clear of our ship; so I alone became their prisoner. They have dealt with me like thieves of mercy: but they knew what they did; I am to do a good turn for them. Let the king have the letters I have sent; and repair thou to me with as much speed as thou wouldst fly death. I have words to speak in thine ear will make thee dumb; yet are they much too light for the bore of the matter. These good fellows will bring thee where I am. Rosencrantz and Guildenstern hold their course for England: of them I have much to tell thee. Farewell.
'He that thou knowest thine, Hamlet.'
Come, I will make you way for these your letters;
And do't the speedier, that you may direct me
To him from whom you brought them.

Exeunt

Act IV Scene VII

Another room in the castle.

Enter KING CLAUDIUS and LAERTES

KING CLAUDIUS   Now must you must put me in your heart for friend,
Sith you have heard that he which hath
Your noble father slain pursued my life.

LAERTES   It well appears: but tell me
Why you proceeded not against these feats.

KING CLAUDIUS   O, for two special reasons; The queen his mother
Lives almost by his looks. The other motive,
Why to a public count I might not go,
Is the great love the general gender bear him.

LAERTES   And so have I a noble father lost;
A sister driven into desperate terms,
but my revenge will come.

KING CLAUDIUS   Break not your sleeps for that: you must not think
That we are made of stuff so flat and dull
That we can let our beard be shook with danger
And think it pastime. You shortly shall hear more:
I loved your father, and we love ourself;
And that, I hope, will teach you to imagine--

Enter a Messenger

How now! what news?

Messenger   Letters, my lord, from Hamlet:
This to your majesty; this to the queen.

KING CLAUDIUS   From Hamlet! who brought them?

Messenger   Sailors, my lord.

KING CLAUDIUS   Laertes, you shall hear them. Leave us.

Exit Messenger

[Reads] 'High and mighty, you shall know I am set naked on
your kingdom. To-morrow shall I beg leave to see
your kingly eyes: when I shall, first asking your
pardon thereunto, recount the occasion of my sudden
and more strange return. 'Hamlet.'

LAERTES
Let him come;
It warms the very sickness in my heart,
That I shall live and tell him to his teeth,
'Thus didest thou.'

KING CLAUDIUS
If it be so, Laertes--
As how should it be so? how otherwise?--
Will you be ruled by me?

LAERTES
Ay, my lord;
So you will not o'errule me to a peace.

KING CLAUDIUS
If he be now return'd, I will work him
To an exploit, now ripe in my device,
Under the which he shall not choose but fall:
And for his death no wind of blame shall breathe,
But even his mother shall call it accident.

LAERTES
My lord, I will be ruled;
The rather, if you could devise it so
That I might be the organ.

KING CLAUDIUS
It falls right.
You have been talk'd of since your travel much,
And that in Hamlet's hearing, for a quality
Wherein, they say, you shine:
Two months since,
Here was a gentleman of Normandy:--
He made confession of you,
And gave you such a masterly report
For art and exercise in your defence
And for your rapier most especially,
That he cried out, 'twould be a sight indeed,
If one could match you: the scrimers of their nation,
He swore, had had neither motion, guard, nor eye,

If you opposed them. Sir, this report of his
Did Hamlet so envenom with his envy
That he could nothing do but wish and beg
Your sudden coming o'er, to play with him.
Now, out of this,--

LAERTES

What out of this, my lord?

KING CLAUDIUS

Laertes, was your father dear to you?
Or are you like the painting of a sorrow,
A face without a heart?

LAERTES

Why ask you this?

KING CLAUDIUS

Not that I think you did not love your father;
But, to the quick o' the ulcer:--
Hamlet comes back: what would you undertake,
To show yourself your father's son in deed
More than in words?

LAERTES

To cut his throat i' the church.

KING CLAUDIUS

No place, indeed, should murder sanctuarize;
Revenge should have no bounds. But, good Laertes,
Hamlet return'd shall know you are come home:
We'll put on those shall praise your excellence
And set a double varnish on the fame
The Frenchman gave you, bring you in fine together
And wager on your heads: he, being remiss,
Most generous and free from all contriving,
Will not peruse the foils; so that, with ease,
Or with a little shuffling, you may choose
A sword unbated, and in a pass of practise
Requite him for your father.

LAERTES

I will do't:
And, for that purpose, I'll anoint my sword.
I bought an unction of a mountebank,
So mortal that, but dip a knife in it,
Where it draws blood no cataplasm so rare,
Can save the thing from death

That is but scratch'd withal: I'll touch my point
With this contagion, that, if I gall him slightly,
It may be death.

KING CLAUDIUS   Let's further think of this; if this should fail,
Through our bad performance, this project
Should have a back or second, that might hold.
I ha't. When in your motion you are hot and dry--
And that he calls for drink, I'll have prepared him
A chalice for the nonce, whereon but sipping,
If he by chance escape your venom'd stuck,
Our purpose may hold there.

Enter QUEEN GERTRUDE

How now, sweet queen!

QUEEN GERTRUDE   One woe doth tread upon another's heel,
So fast they follow; your sister's drown'd, Laertes.

LAERTES   Drown'd! O, where?

QUEEN GERTRUDE   There is a willow grows aslant a brook,
That shows his hoar leaves in the glassy stream;
There with fantastic garlands did she come
Of crow-flowers, nettles, daisies, and long purples
That liberal shepherds give a grosser name,
But our cold maids do dead men's fingers call them:
There, on the pendent boughs her coronet weeds
Clambering to hang, an envious sliver broke;
When down her weedy trophies and herself
Fell in the weeping brook. Her clothes spread wide;
And, mermaid-like, awhile they bore her up:
Which time she chanted snatches of old tunes;
As one incapable of her own distress,
Or like a creature native and indued
Unto that element: but long it could not be
Till that her garments, heavy with their drink,
Pull'd the poor wretch from her melodious lay
To muddy death.

LAERTES   Too much of water hast thou, poor Ophelia,
And therefore I forbid my tears: but yet
It is our trick; nature her custom holds,
Let shame say what it will: when these are gone,
The woman will be out. Adieu, my lord:
I have a speech of fire, that fain would blaze,
But that this folly douts it.

Exit

KING CLAUDIUS   Let's follow, Gertrude:
How much I had to do to calm his rage!
Now fear I this will give it start again;
Therefore let's follow.

Exeunt

Act V

Act V Scene I

A churchyard.

Enter two Clowns, with spades, & c

First Clown   Is she to be buried in Christian burial that wilfully seeks her own salvation?

Second Clown   I tell thee she is: and therefore make her grave straight.

First Clown   How can that be, unless she drowned herself in her own defence?

Second Clown   Will you ha' the truth on't? If this had not been a gentlewoman, she should have been buried out o' Christian burial.

First Clown   Why, there thou say'st. I'll put another question to thee.

Second Clown   Go to.

First Clown   What is he that builds stronger than either the mason, the shipwright, or the carpenter?

Second Clown   'Who builds stronger than a mason, a shipwright, or a carpenter?' Mass, I cannot tell.

Enter HAMLET and HORATIO, at a distance

First Clown   Cudgel thy brains no more about it, for your dull ass will not mend his pace with beating; and, when you are asked this question next, say 'a grave-maker: 'the houses that he makes last till doomsday. Go, fetch me a stoup of liquor.

Exit Second Clown. He digs throws up a skull

HAMLET   Why may not that be the skull of a lawyer?

	Why does he suffer this rude knave Now to knock him about the sconce with a dirty shovel, And will not tell him of his action of battery? Hum! I will speak to this fellow. Whose grave's this, sirrah?
First Clown	Mine, sir.
HAMLET	I think it be thine, indeed; for thou liest in't.
First Clown	You lie out on't, sir, and therefore it is not yours: for my part, I do not lie in't, and yet it is mine.
HAMLET	'Thou dost lie in't, to be in't and say it is thine: 'tis for the dead, not for the quick; therefore thou liest. What man dost thou dig it for?
First Clown	For no man, sir.
HAMLET	What woman, then?
First Clown	One that was a woman, sir; but, rest her soul, she's dead.
HAMLET	How absolute the knave is Horatio. How long hast thou been a grave-maker?
First Clown	Of all the days i' the year, I came to't that day that our last king Hamlet overcame Fortinbras. it was the very day that young Hamlet was born; he that is mad, and sent into England.
HAMLET	Ay, marry, why was he sent into England?
First Clown	Why, because he was mad: he shall recover his wits there; or, if he do not, it's no great matter, there the men are as mad as he.
HAMLET	How long will a man lie i' the earth ere he rot?
First Clown	I' faith, if he be not rotten before he die--as we have many pocky corses now-a-days, he will last you some eight year or nine year. Here's a skull now; this skull has lain in the earth three and twenty years.
HAMLET	Whose was it?

First Clown   A whoreson mad fellow's it was: This same skull,
sir, was Yorick's skull, the king's jester.

HAMLET   This? Let me see.

Takes the skull

Alas, poor Yorick! I knew him, Horatio: a fellow
of infinite jest, of most excellent fancy: he hath
borne me on his back a thousand times; and now, how
abhorred in my imagination it is! my gorge rims at
it. Here hung those lips that I have kissed I know
not how oft. Where be your gibes now? your
gambols? your songs? your flashes of merriment,
that were wont to set the table on a roar? Not one
now, to mock your own grinning? quite chap-fallen?
Prithee, Horatio, tell me one thing.
Dost thou think Alexander looked o' this fashion i'
the earth? And smelt so? pah!

Puts down the skull

HORATIO   E'en so, my lord.

HAMLET   To what base uses we may return, Horatio! Why may
not imagination trace the noble dust of Alexander,
till he find it stopping a bung-hole?
Alexander died, Alexander was buried,
Alexander returneth into dust; the dust is earth; of
earth we make loam; and why of that loam,
might they not stop a beer-barrel?
But soft! but soft! aside: here comes the king.

Enter Priest, & c. in procession; the Corpse of OPHELIA, LAERTES and Mourners following; KING CLAUDIUS, QUEEN GERTRUDE, their trains, & c

The queen, the courtiers: who is this they follow?
And with such maimed rites? This doth betoken
the corse they follow did with desperate hand
fordo its own life: 'twas of some estate.
Couch we awhile, and mark.

Retiring with HORATIO

74

LAERTES	What ceremony else?
First Priest	Her obsequies have been as far enlarged As we have warrantise: her death was doubtful; And, but that great command o'ersways the order, She should in ground unsanctified have lodged.
LAERTES	Lay her i' the earth: I tell thee, churlish priest, A ministering angel shall my sister be, When thou liest howling.
HAMLET	What, the fair Ophelia!
QUEEN GERTRUDE	Sweets to the sweet: farewell!

Scattering flowers

	I hoped thou shouldst have been my Hamlet's wife.
LAERTES	O, treble woe Fall ten times treble on that cursed head, Whose wicked deed thy most ingenious sense Deprived thee of! Hold off the earth awhile, Till I have caught her once more in mine arms:

Leaps into the grave

HAMLET	*[Advancing]* What is he whose grief Bears such an emphasis? whose phrase of sorrow Conjures the wandering stars, and makes them stand Like wonder-wounded hearers? This is I, Hamlet the Dane.

Leaps into the grave

LAERTES	The devil take thy soul!

Grappling with him

HAMLET	I prithee, take thy fingers from my throat; hold off thy hand.
KING CLAUDIUS	Pluck them asunder.

The Attendants part them, and they come out of the grave

HAMLET   Why I will fight with him upon this theme
Until my eyelids will no longer wag.

QUEEN GERTRUDE   O my son, what theme?

HAMLET   I loved Ophelia: forty thousand brothers
Could not, with all their quantity of love,
Make up my sum. What wilt thou do for her?

KING CLAUDIUS   O, he is mad, Laertes.

QUEEN GERTRUDE   For love of God, forbear him.

HAMLET   'Swounds, show me what thou'lt do:
Woo't weep? woo't fight? woo't fast? woo't tear thyself?
Woo't drink up eisel? eat a crocodile?
I'll do't. Dost thou come here to whine?
To outface me with leaping in her grave?
Be buried quick with her, and so will I!

QUEEN GERTRUDE   This is mere madness.

HAMLET   Hear you, sir;
What is the reason that you use me thus?
I loved you ever: but it is no matter;
Let Hercules himself do what he may,
The cat will mew and dog will have his day.

Exit

KING CLAUDIUS   I pray you, good Horatio, wait upon him.

Exit HORATIO. To LAERTES

Strengthen your patience in our last night's speech;
We'll put the matter to the present push.
Good Gertrude, set some watch over your son.

Exeunt

Act V Scene II

A hall in the castle.

Enter HAMLET and HORATIO

HAMLET	Sir: now shall you see. Up from my cabin,
	My sea-gown scarf'd about me, in the dark
	Groped I to find out them; had my desire.
	Making so bold to unseal their grand commission;
	Where I found, Horatio,-- O royal knavery!
	An exact command,
	That, not to stay the grinding of the axe,
	My head should be struck off.
HORATIO	Is't possible?
HAMLET	Here's the commission: read it at more leisure.
	But wilt thou hear me how I did proceed?
HORATIO	I beseech you.
HAMLET	Being thus be-netted round with villanies,--
	I devised a new commission,
	An earnest conjuration from the king,
	That, on the view and knowing of these contents,
	He should the bearers put to sudden death,
	Not shriving-time allow'd. Now, the next day
	Was our sea-fight; and what to this was sequent
	Thou know'st already.
HORATIO	So Guildenstern and Rosencrantz go to't.
HAMLET	Why, man, they did make love to this employment;
	They are not near my conscience; their defeat
	Does by their own insinuation grow
HORATIO	Why, what a king is this!
HAMLET	Does it not, think'st thee, stand me now upon--
	He that hath kill'd my king and whored my mother,
	Popp'd in between the election and my hopes,
	Thrown out his angle for my proper life,

And with such cozenage--is't not perfect conscience,
To quit him with this arm? and is't not to be damn'd,
To let this canker of our nature come
In further evil?

HORATIO   It must be shortly known to him from England
What is the issue of the business there.

HAMLET   It will be short: the interim is mine;
But I am very sorry, good Horatio,
That to Laertes I forgot myself;
I'll court his favours. The bravery of his grief did put me
Into a towering passion.

HORATIO   Peace! who comes here?

Enter OSRIC

OSRIC   Your lordship is right welcome back to Denmark.

HAMLET   I humbly thank you, sir. Dost know this water-fly?

HORATIO   No, my good lord.

HAMLET   Thy state is the more gracious; for 'tis a vice to
know him.

OSRIC   Sweet lord, if your lordship were at leisure, I
should impart a thing to you from his majesty.

HAMLET   I will receive it, sir, with all diligence of
spirit.

OSRIC   My lord, his majesty bade me signify to you
that he has laid a great wager on your head:
Sir, here is newly come to court Laertes.

HAMLET   Well, sir?

OSRIC   You are not ignorant of what excellence Laertes is--
I mean, sir, for his weapon.

HAMLET   What's his weapon?

OSRIC	Rapier and dagger.
HAMLET	That's two of his weapons: but, well.
OSRIC	The king, sir, hath wagered with him six Barbary horses: against the which he has imponed, as I take it, six French rapiers and poniards, with their assigns.
HAMLET	Why is this 'imponed,' as you call it?
OSRIC	The king, sir, hath laid, that in a dozen passes between yourself and him, he shall not exceed you three hits: he hath laid on twelve for nine; and it would come to immediate trial, if your lordship would vouchsafe the answer.
HAMLET	Sir, let the foils be brought, the gentleman willing, and the king hold his purpose, I will win for him an I can; if not, I will gain nothing but my shame and the odd hits.
OSRIC	I commend my duty to your lordship.

Exit OSRIC. Enter a Lord

Lord	My lord, his majesty sends to know if your pleasure hold to play with Laertes, or that you will take longer time.
HAMLET	If his fitness speaks, mine is ready.
Lord	The queen desires you to use some gentle entertainment to Laertes before you fall to play.
HAMLET	She well instructs me.

Exit Lord

HORATIO	You will lose this wager, my lord.
HAMLET	I do not think so: since he went into France, I have been in continual practise: I shall win at the

odds. But thou wouldst not think how ill all's here
about my heart: but it is no matter.

HORATIO   Nay, good my lord, If your mind dislike any thing,
obey it: I will say you are not fit.

HAMLET   Not a whit, we defy augury: there's a special
providence in the fall of a sparrow. If it be now,
'tis not to come; if it be not to come, it will be
now; if it be not now, yet it will come: the
readiness is all: since no man has aught of what he
leaves, what is't to leave betimes?

Enter KING CLAUDIUS, QUEEN GERTRUDE, LAERTES, Lords, OSRIC, and Attendants with foils, & c

KING CLAUDIUS   Come, Hamlet, come, and take this hand from me.

KING CLAUDIUS puts LAERTES' hand into HAMLET's

HAMLET   Give me your pardon, sir: I've done you wrong;
But pardon't, as you are a gentleman.
What I have done, I here proclaim was madness.
Was't Hamlet wrong'd Laertes? Never Hamlet:
If Hamlet from himself be ta'en away,
Then Hamlet does it not.

LAERTES   I am satisfied in nature,
Whose motive, in this case, should stir me most
To my revenge: but in my terms of honour
I stand aloof; and do receive your offer'd love like love,
And will not wrong it.

HAMLET   I embrace it freely;
And will this brother's wager frankly play.
Give us the foils. Come on.

LAERTES   Come, one for me.

They prepare to play

KING CLAUDIUS   Set me the stoops of wine upon that table.
The king shall drink to Hamlet's better breath;

And in the cup an union shall he throw,
Richer than that which four successive kings
In Denmark's crown have worn. Give me the cups;
Come, begin.

HAMLET Come on, sir.

LAERTES Come, my lord.

They play

HAMLET One.

LAERTES No.

HAMLET Judgment.

OSRIC A hit, a very palpable hit.

LAERTES Well; again.

KING CLAUDIUS Stay; give me drink. Hamlet, this pearl is thine;
Here's to thy health.

Trumpets sound, and cannon shot off within

Give him the cup.

HAMLET I'll play this bout first; set it by awhile. Come.

They play

Another hit; what say you?

LAERTES A touch, a touch, I do confess.

KING CLAUDIUS Our son shall win.

QUEEN GERTRUDE The queen carouses to thy fortune, Hamlet.

KING CLAUDIUS Gertrude, do not drink.

QUEEN GERTRUDE I will, my lord; I pray you, pardon me.

KING CLAUDIUS   [Aside] It is the poison'd cup: it is too late.

HAMLET   I dare not drink yet, madam; by and by.

QUEEN GERTRUDE   Come, let me wipe thy face.

LAERTES   My lord, I'll hit him now.

KING CLAUDIUS   I do not think't.

LAERTES   [Aside] And yet 'tis almost 'gainst my conscience.

HAMLET   Come, for the third, Laertes: you but dally;
                      I pray you, pass with your best violence.

They play

LAERTES   Have at you now!

LAERTES wounds HAMLET; then in scuffling, they exchange rapiers, and HAMLET wounds LAERTES

KING CLAUDIUS   Part them; they are incensed.

HAMLET   Nay, come, again.

QUEEN GERTRUDE falls

OSRIC   Look to the queen there, ho!

HORATIO   They bleed on both sides. How is it, my lord?

OSRIC   How is't, Laertes?

LAERTES   Why, as a woodcock to mine own springe, Osric;
                      I am justly kill'd with mine own treachery.

HAMLET   How does the queen?

KING CLAUDIUS   She swounds to see them bleed.

QUEEN GERTRUDE   No, no, the drink, the drink,--O my dear Hamlet,--
                      The drink, the drink! I am poison'd. *[Dies]*

HAMLET	O villany! Ho! let the door be lock'd: Treachery! Seek it out.
LAERTES	It is here, Hamlet: Hamlet, thou art slain; No medicine in the world can do thee good; The treacherous instrument is in thy hand, Unbated and envenom'd: the foul practise Hath turn'd itself on me lo, here I lie, Never to rise again: thy mother's poison'd: I can no more: the king, the king's to blame.
HAMLET	The point!--envenom'd too! Then, venom, to thy work.

Stabs KING CLAUDIUS

All	Treason! treason!
KING CLAUDIUS	O, yet defend me, friends; I am but hurt.
HAMLET	Here, thou incestuous, murderous, damned Dane, Drink off this potion. Is thy union here? Follow my mother.

KING CLAUDIUS dies

LAERTES	He is justly served; It is a poison temper'd by himself. Exchange forgiveness with me, noble Hamlet: Mine and my father's death come not upon thee, Nor thine on me. *[Dies]*
HAMLET	Heaven make thee free of it! I follow thee. I am dead, Horatio. Thou livest; Report me and my cause aright To the unsatisfied.
HORATIO	Never believe it: I am more an antique Roman than a Dane: Here's yet some liquor left.
HAMLET	As thou'rt a man, Give me the cup: let go. O good Horatio,

What a wounded name shall live behind me!
If thou didst ever hold me in thy heart
Draw thy breath in pain to tell my story.

March afar off, and shot within

What warlike noise is this?

OSRIC Young Fortinbras, with conquest come from Poland.

HAMLET O, I die, Horatio;
But I do prophesy the election lights
On Fortinbras: he has my dying voice;
So tell him, with the occurrents, more and less,
Which have solicited. The rest is silence. *[Dies]*

HORATIO Now cracks a noble heart. Good night sweet prince:
And flights of angels sing thee to thy rest!
Why does the drum come hither?

March within. Enter FORTINBRAS, the English Ambassadors, and others

PRINCE FORTINBRAS O proud death,
What feast is toward in thine eternal cell,
That thou so many princes at a shot
So bloodily hast struck?

HORATIO You from the Polack wars, give order that these bodies
High on a stage be placed to the view;
And let me speak to the yet unknowing world
How these things came about: so shall you hear
Of carnal, bloody, and unnatural acts,
Of accidental judgments, casual slaughters,
Of deaths put on by cunning and forced cause,
And, in this upshot, purposes mistook
Fall'n on the inventors' heads: all this can I
Truly deliver.

PRINCE FORTINBRAS Let us haste to hear it,
And call the noblest to the audience.
For me, with sorrow I embrace my fortune:

I have some rights of memory in this kingdom,
Which now to claim my vantage doth invite me.

PRINCE FORTINBRAS Let four captains
Bear Hamlet, like a soldier, to the stage;
For he was likely, had he been put on,
To have proved most royally:
Take up the bodies: such a sight as this
Becomes the field, but here shows much amiss.
Go, bid the soldiers shoot.

A dead march. Exeunt, bearing off the dead bodies; after which a peal of ordnance is shot off.

Shakespeare Abridged for Schools and Performance

Other books in the series:

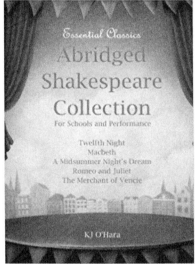

Printed in Great Britain
by Amazon

22069872R00053